YOUR KNOWLEDGE H

- We will publish your bachelor's and master's thesis, essays and papers

- Your own eBook and book - sold worldwide in all relevant shops

- Earn money with each sale

Upload your text at www.GRIN.com and publish for free

Thuy Nguyen

Political correctness in the English language

GRIN Verlag

Bibliografische Information der Deutschen Nationalbibliothek:

Die Deutsche Bibliothek verzeichnet diese Publikation in der Deutschen National-
bibliografie; detaillierte bibliografische Daten sind im Internet über http://dnb.d-
nb.de/ abrufbar.

Imprint:

Copyright © 2007 GRIN Verlag GmbH
Druck und Bindung: Books on Demand GmbH, Norderstedt Germany
ISBN: 978-3-640-18157-5

This book at GRIN:

http://www.grin.com/en/e-book/115796/political-correctness-in-the-english-language

GRIN - Your knowledge has value

Der GRIN Verlag publiziert seit 1998 wissenschaftliche Arbeiten von Studenten, Hochschullehrern und anderen Akademikern als eBook und gedrucktes Buch. Die Verlagswebsite www.grin.com ist die ideale Plattform zur Veröffentlichung von Hausarbeiten, Abschlussarbeiten, wissenschaftlichen Aufsätzen, Dissertationen und Fachbüchern.

Visit us on the internet:

http://www.grin.com/

http://www.facebook.com/grincom

http://www.twitter.com/grin_com

Universität Duisburg Essen
Fachbereich Anglistik
Sommersemester 2007
Seminar: Language and Gender

Political Correctness in the English Language

Thuy Nguyen

Contents

1. Introduction

In London during the 1980ies there were reports in the right-wing press, that socialist local councils like Hackney Council had to banish the word *manhole* by order of its Women's Committee since the term was meant to be sexist. This is just one out of many incidences that came up during the political correctness debate. Since the eighties this phenomenon has occurred on the American campuses and developed rapidly to a publicly debated subject. This essay will deal with the phenomenon of the political correctness in the English language with the main focus on gender questions and feminist linguistics. The central question is if expressions like *policemen* or phrases like to *be the master of the situation* are really conceived as sexist by the majority of people and if replacing those by terms like "police officers" can solve the problem of sexist language use. Have the efforts to regulate or reform language been successful and can language be at all non-sexist or even neutral?

First of all, the term political correctness and politically correct are placed into a historical context explaining its roots and development before trying to define the concept. Furthermore, the importance of the political correctness debate for the Women's Liberation Movement and the development of feminist linguistics will be explained.

The third chapter explains on which assumptions and theories the claimed language change is based on. The relation between language use and perception of the individual or of a group plays a central part. In the context of the political correctness debate the central question is in how far sexist language use, representation, the naming or not naming of women effects the perception and thinking of people.

The fourth chapter gives a description of the measures that were taken in order to influence language and language use. On the one hand, measures aimed at the regulation and sanction of sexist language and on the other hand, some more moderate and liberal measures intended the reformation of language in order to achieve more equality between women and men on a linguistic level. In how far have these measures been successful in increasing the awareness for discriminating language use?

2. Definition and historical background

2.1 Political correctness

2.1.1 Historical development of the terms *Political Correctness* and *Political Correct*

According to Cameron (Greil 1998:7) the term political correctness as a noun first appeared in the eighties in the course of the debate about Political Correctness in the USA, especially on the American Universities. Until then the adjective politically correct was mainly used. The distinction of those terms is of importance since it reveals the development of an adjective that expresses and judges the behaviour of an individual or a group to a noun that refers to an existing phenomenon. Political Correctness is perceived by the American public as a movement and a social phenomenon located on university campuses and political or cultural institutions such as feminist, racist or leftist organizations.

The term "politically incorrect" was suggested to have derived from Marxist-Leninist vocabulary in order to describe the appropriate party line commonly referred to as the "correct line". According to Perry (Cameron 1995: 126) the phrase was adopted from the translation of Mao Tse –Tung's *Red Book*. Regardless of the different sources the term politically correct can in this context be understood as conformity to official policy.

In the late sixties and seventies the term was taken up again in the course of reform and Civil Rights movements by American New Left activists, Afro-Americans and feminist groups. It was also understood as insider expression with the function to satirize the group's own tendency towards humourless, rigid and orthodox Right party line. The term was therefore often used with a sarcastic and an ironic meaning by Lefts while conservative opponents of PC used it with a pejorative connotation.

During the late eighties, the term political correctness and his keywords have according to Cameron (1995) underlain a discursive drift meaning that it begins to drift away from its earlier meaning since it has been taken up in the mass media. At the beginning debate in the USA around 1987 the term was used in connection with particular issues concerning university curricula, speech codes and affirmative actions. However, it was brought up in the media rather detached from its present context and thus the public developed a very general idea of the term political correctness. While those political groups who were directly engaged in the debate related concrete ideas, objectives and measures like speech regulations to the issue, large parts of the public who were not actively involved in the debate related the term rather to the creation of neologisms whose meaning has to be concluded from the context.

Consequently, the term has due to the process of discursive drift and the massive public perception of the phenomenon developed to a catchword or slogan attracting public and media attention and which can be used in nearly every context.

2.1.2 Definition

It is nearly impossible to give an exact definition of the terms "political correctness" and its adjective "politically correct" since they were and are still used in many different contexts and as it had been already explained in the previous chapter it had been subject to discursive drift.

However, there is no doubt that political correctness refers to the political movement and phenomenon, which began in the USA, with the aim to enforce a set of ideologies and views on gender, race and other minorities. Political correctness refers to language and ideas that may cause offence to some identity groups like women and aims at giving preferential treatment to members of those social groups in schools and universities. The reformation of language is within the political correctness debate the central topic with the aim to undermine sexist or racist expressions either by speech codes or by replacing words, which are on the index, by new ones.

Consequently, a number of neologisms have developed that are simply grotesque or have the aim to provoke. By changing the term *history* into *herstory* feminists try to draw attention to the under -representation of women in the history (Schenz 1994:25). Another purpose of the movement is the construction of educational curricula, in which the traditional idea of cultural heritage being determined by "dead white males" is replaced by putting the emphasis on non-western, non-white and female contribution. In addition, these curricula recommend the kind of language which is appropriate to use when talking about gender and racial differences.

Political Correctness has above all the aim to regulate language and behaviour in order to prevent minorities from discrimination, to reduce prejudices and take the cultural diversity and heterogeneity of the American society into consideration.

2.2 Women's Liberation Movement and Feminist linguistic criticism

The feminist linguistic criticism, which occurred during the Women's Liberation Movement in the 1960ies, has led to the most extensive language change up to present and to a more sensitive and conscious language use. The Women's Liberation Movement aimed at the elimination of each form of oppression based on gender and wanted to achieve an equal economic and social status for women. The prevalent language use reflecting the social situation of women was regarded as one central form of oppression since "sexist language teaches us what those who use it [...] think women's place to be: second class citizens, neither seen nor heard, external sexobjects and personifications of evil." (Cameron in Wierlemann 2002: 63)

The feminist linguistics assumed that language influences consciousness and perception. Due to this assumption they intended the formulation of a critical linguistics in order to initiate the change of language use, which would finally result in the change of consciousness. To facilitate language change, an analysis of the current language use was essential. In their analysis the adherents of feminist linguistics came to the conclusion that the prevalent language use reflected sexism and is discriminating. Whereas this kind of language use might be considered to be a symptom for a general, possibly unconscious impoliteness or rudeness people possess. And since sex discrimination might not be conscious, it is possible to make the speaker aware of his or her careless language use.

Feminist linguistics did not only condemn sexist language use but the English language system with its generic pronouns. The problem of common gender and the alternative proposals will be further discussed in chapter 3.2.

However, some efforts of the feminist linguistics were regarded as quite controversial such as the claim that the word *history* would be understood as **his***tory* dominated and determined by male. The alternative proposal *herstory* would value and emphasize the contributions and meaning of women whereas it is disregarded that there is no etymological connection between the word *history* and the pronoun *his.* (Wierlemann 2002:66) Similar proposals like *sefemtics, femtal* or *hufem* were due to those etymologically wrong conclusions not taken serious.

Finally, Cameron maintains that it was the aim of the Women's Liberation Movement to strive for a sensitised language use, a "non-sexist language [...] which excludes neither women nor men" (Wierlemann 1985:68). Its proponents wanted to consider the social change that was initiated by the reform movement as well in the language use, which they to some extent could achieve with the neutralisation of gender-specific terms by changing terms like *chairman* into *chairperson* or *chair*. The ideas of the Women's Liberation Movement are still present today and the main achievement of its proponents is that they have initiated and mobilized the public discussion in society which has finally led to a change in the language use.

3. Language and thinking: Explaining the need for a language change

3.1 The Sapir-Whorf-hypothesis

The politically motivated language change above all by feminists assumes that "language is not just a medium for ideas but also a shaper of ideas" (Cameron 1995:122). The assumption that there is a relation between language and ideas of a society, known as the principle of linguistic relativity, has already been discussed in the context of the controversial linguistic concept known as the Sapir- Whorf – hypothesis. In the 1930ies the linguist Edward Sapir and his colleague and student Benjamin Whorf claimed that there is a systematic relationship between the grammatical categories of the language a person speaks and the way this person understands the worlds and his behaviour in it. Consequently, not only society and culture influence language but the nature of language itself has an immense impact on habitual thought and perception of the individual and therefore on society and its culture.

In Whorf's words "we dissect nature along lines laid down by our natives language"(Yule 1996:247) meaning that speakers of different languages would have due to the differences of their mother tongue a diverse view of the world whereas Whorf emphasizes that there are no suchlike discrepancies between the modern European languages since they would display great structural similarities (Greil

1998:106). In the course of language acquisition the perception of the world, its construction and organisation is significantly influenced by linguistic structures. Consequently, the diverse structures of different languages would lead to different descriptions of the world and therefore to different perceptions native speakers of these languages have.

These arguments are used by political correctness proponents to explain and defend their claim for a necessary language change. If language reflects and shapes the society to which it is linked, sexist and discriminating language use would therefore not only reflect but also shape and construct a sexist and discriminating society.

Consequently, successful language policy that would initiate and assert a more sensitive language change would finally result in social and cultural changes. Measures like speech codes or guidelines aim at initiating a language change to assert more cultural sensitivity in language use and therefore eliminate discriminations towards women.

3.2 The common gender/generic masculine

There have been many efforts to prove the validity of the principle of linguistic relativity, which has been described in the previous chapter. In 1993 Brigitte Scheele and Eva Gauler studied the validity of this concept in reference to the relation between gender and sexuality in the linguistic system (Greil 1998:108). The justification of feminist criticism would depend on if and in how far there would be empirical evidence for Whorf's theory. The central question Scheele/Gauler pursued was in how far the linguistic representation and non-naming of women would influence the perception of them.

Feminist linguistic criticism did not only denounce language use but the language as a system as well. According to feminist critique there are linguistic phenomena in the form of discriminating metaphors that influence the perception of women. Amongst these sexist metaphors the common gender or generic masculine has established in the everyday language of English. A generic term or common gender is used to refer to a majority of nouns, which are independent from gender like *survivor* or *author*. The main criticism by feminists is that women would not be made visible by the use common gender although it does either refer to precisely to

8

men. However, several empirical studies like the one of Scheele/Gauler have revealed that it is rather uncommon that women are meant when using gender neutral expressions. This shows that the concept of *women* is theoretically not as present as the concept of *man.*

The use of generic masculine would manifest a view of the world in which the masculine represents the norm in metaphoric expressions like to "be master of a situation". Feminist groups claim that children would acquire aspects of this dominant worldview while acquiring language. In gender marked languages like English, French and German, the masculine form is used to refer to several persons of both sexes. For the English language there have been numerous studies concerning mainly the use of generic *man* and the masculine pronouns *he/his/him* in gender neutral contexts since English nouns and especially job titles like *typist, student* or *judge* are compared to German terms like *Richter* or *Richterin*) in general gender-neutral.

Nevertheless, studies have confirmed that most people refer *he*, although used in gender-neutral contexts, only to men. Sentences like *a doctor is a busy person, he must be able to balance a million obligations at once* imply that all doctors are men (Jacobsen o.J.). Since *he* is read by many as a masculine pronoun, especially women have come to feel that generic pronouns exclude women. The alternative that has been proposed in order to avoid discriminating effects of the generic masculine is the substitution of *man* by *person* or replacement of generic *he* by plural forms like *they*, which is also used as 3rd person singular form although it is not grammatically correct. An example taken from the *Guidelines for Gender-Fair Use of Language* reveals that this construction is becoming increasingly acceptable. A proposed alternative to the statement "does each student have his book" is then "does each student have their book?"

Another alternative is the use of double-pronoun constructions meaning that "he/she" or "his/her" are used in one sentence whereas the order, in which the pronouns are used, is also of importance. Further inclusive forms are the pluralizing of pronouns as well as the elimination of exclusive pronouns.

According to the *Guidelines for Gender-Fair Use of Language* edited by the WILLA (Women In Literacy and Life Assembly) the generic use of the noun *man* to represent both women and men excludes women and "minimalizes their contributions and worth as human beings". Suggested alternatives to terms like *man* or *mankind*s are *humanity, human beings* or *people.*

Finally, several studies like those of Scheele/Gauler have confirmed that the use of generic masculine has an exclusive effect and that language can be discriminating. However, the proposed alternatives do not automatically result in the better perception and inclusion of women. Therefore, the generic masculine cannot be regarded as the main cause for the male interpretation of nouns in generic and gender- neutral contexts. This leads to the conclusion that language has an influence on the perception and cognition but does not determine them.

4. Measures of political correctness: Speech codes and language reforms

4.1 Speech codes

During the eighties there were several efforts at the American Colleges and Universities to sensitize the academic staff and the students for the problem of discrimination and the cultural diversity. This can finally be understood as a reaction to the increasing complaints about issues of sexual harassment. In the context of the Antidiscrimination campaign some universities aimed at the improvement of the situation on a linguistic level.

One measure that has been adopted in the context of this campaign was the exclusion and sanction of *harassing* and *offensive language,* meaning the verbal pestering and the use of insulting language use towards certain persons or groups (Greil 1998:46). Language regulations as an integrated part of the *codes of conduct* for students and the university personnel, which have the aim to undermine the use of so-called *hate speech* by sanctions, are called *speech codes.* Speech Codes cannot be understood as the prohibition of single lexemes or phrases; they occur in the form of short and general statements, which do not allow the expression of discriminating comments and insults towards other persons. Expressions, which are commonly regarded to be insulting and offensive towards a single person with regard to his/her gender, race or ethnicity and which have the aim to incite hatred and violence, are defined as *fighting words* (Greil 1998:48). Fighting words as well as hate speech concern the particular field of tabooed language and language use.

With the introduction of speech codes and the prohibition of fighting words and hate speech universities want to achieve that all students have the possibility to take part in programmes and activities in "a working and learning environment which is free from sexual harassment" (Greil 1998:235). Sexual harassment expresses among others in

> […]statements which communicate to students or employees limiting preconceptions about appropriate and expected behaviours, abilities, career directions, and personal goals which are based on sex rather than individual interest or ability. (Greil 1998:235)

4.1.1 Legitimation of speech regulations

There are several reasons that proponents of PC support and defend speech codes and language regulations. One explanation is based on a specific interpretation of the First Amendment, which among others guarantees the freedom of speech. According to Raymond Hunthausen, an archbishop from Seattle, this freedom is rather limited:

> […] It is good that all people are finally free to express their ideas, and we rely on reason to help us sort the wisdom from the folly. But we must never forget those times that reason has failed us, that language has slid ridiculous to inflammatory, inciting riots and violence detrimental to the common good. Freedom of expression does not mean that all speech is protected, and drawing the lines is admittedly hard. (Schenz 1994:41)

As soon as freedom of speech is abused e.g. by sexist or racist people to insult others or to instigate violence, language regulations would be obligatory. The increasing numbers of sexist and racist incidences or so-called hate crimes, which mainly resulted from verbal insults, make speech regulations in the eyes of its proponents indispensable in order to prevent concerned groups from such incidents. According to the proponents of political correctness the university has the moral duty to work against such incidents and therefore speech regulations were regarded as the logical consequence of these occurrences. Finally, these measures have the function to re-establish the social morality and to increase the sensitivity and awareness for the concerned groups or individuals.

4.1.2 Arguments against speech regulations

Due to internal controversies on the universities and due to many court decisions it was agreed that "no particular language can be declared punishable in advance "(Friedmann 1995:3) and that it must be proved that fighting words entail a "clear and present danger of a breach of peace, for instance, a violent reaction by the insulted party" as Friedmann maintains. According to Cameron it is on a linguistic level very difficult to label single words as dangerous since therefore it is necessary to know "what this or that expression really means" (Cameron 1995:157) and in how far single lexemes have a negative and insulting connotation. The problem is that the negative connotation of a word cannot be determined independently from the context it is actually used in. An offence is not inherent in a particular piece of language but it is also established by contextualized acts of language use whereas the choice of words may be relevant to this act.

An additional problem and the cause for the public controversy about speech codes is that in the opinion of many critics the institution of speech codes is not consistent with the freedom of speech and press, which is guaranteed in the First Amendment of the American Constitution. Speech codes would create an atmosphere, in which students are afraid to take part in discussions on controversial topics since they could be denunciated as sexist.

Furthermore, there is also disagreement within the affected groups e.g. women concerning speech codes. Although the majority of affected groups support the idea to be protected from discrimination and having the option to lodge a complaint, several students consider that discrimination is also existent apart from the university campus and that they have to learn to cope with it. As a consequence, speech codes exist due to heavy resistance and several court decisions in a very modified and restricted form.

4.2. Guidelines for non–sexist language

4.2.1 Development and purpose

While speech codes as a political measure include the prohibition and sanction of discriminating language use in predominantly spoken language, other measures have the aim to encourage inclusive and non-discriminatory language use on the one hand and on the other hand to raise consciousness for the often hidden discrimination through language. These kinds of measures do not aim like speech codes at the sanction of verbal aggression towards special people but concentrate mainly on written and public language with the aim to achieve equal treatment of all persons on a linguistic level and to reduce the use of sexist language. Guidelines were originally created to work against the linguistic discrimination in job offers. Discrimination in job offers was a problem that gained attention in the seventies after the Civil Right Act in 1964 had come into force, which prohibited among others the discrimination of employees with regard to gender. Due to several court decisions job offers had to contain information with demands that refer explicitly to the competence of an applicant. It was not allowed to exclude certain groups, like women, by positions offered. Offers, which explicitly demanded female or male applicants or used gender-specific titles like *waitress* or *salesman,* were regarded as an offence towards *equal employment opportunities* (Greil 1998:60). In order to support companies with the design of their job advertisements, guidelines for sex-inclusive language use were developed by public institutions. Nevertheless, language reform did not only affected text sorts like job advertisements, after some time other public institutions and publishing houses felt pressure to eliminate sexist language use from their publications, especially from teaching material and school books.

4.2.2 The Handbook of Non-Sexist Writing

Such a moderate and liberal approach to reform language can be seen in the work of Casey Miller and Kate Swift whose *Handbook of Non-Sexist Writing* (1981) has served as a helpful guide for journalists for many years. According to Cameron (1992:103) for Miller and Swift, the major problem with sexist language was that it was outdated and only existed as a habit that most of the people were used to to follow. The idea behind these guidelines was that language practices needed to be changed in order to bring about fairer representation of different groups since it is the business of language to represent reality. And therefore it is necessary to modify language or even invent new terms where old ones will not do (Goddard 2000:74). Miller and Swift gave their main attention to the following areas:

1. The use of "man" as false generic
As already described in previous chapters, generic terms are applicable to a class or a group and to its individual members. The word men has once been a generic term

meaning person or human being and was equally applicable to either sex. However, writers who persist in using man in its original sense nowadays are often misunderstood by their readers since they associate man with male. As a result, women feel excluded by the use of man with a general meaning. Miller and Swift have presented several alternatives to the "generic" man:

- Replacing man by generalizations like someone, anyone, no one
- Replacing terms like mankind and forefathers by ancestors or human beings
- man as prefix as in manpower are replaced by terms like human resources or workforce
- man as suffix as in tradesman, chairman, salesman are replaced by terms like tradesperson, chair, salesperson

2. The pronoun problem (see chapter 3.2)

3. Discriminating job titles

Most of the job titles derive from a time when only males performed the jobs described. Nowadays women have the option to perform the same jobs as men do and the other way round, which makes old job titles, when they are retained, discriminatory. Although employers advertise positions as being open to both sexes, they keep the old sex-labelled titles. According to Miller/Swift (1981:38) these titles act like a code, psychologically inhibiting women from applying for such jobs as foreman. In addition, job titles like junior executive encourage age discrimination. Consequently; the United States Department of Labor has modified its Dictionary of occupation in order to eliminate sexism as well as ageism. Examples taken from the Department of Labor Job Titles Revisions from 1975 (Goddard 2000:74) are:

Original term	New term
airline steward, stewardess	flight attendant
foreman	supervisor
cameraman	camera operator
fireman	firefighter
policeman	police officer

office girl, boy	office helper
junior executive	executive trainee
housewife	house manager

Although many common-gender job titles have been accepted they are not necessarily being used routinely and others were resisted by some people or organizations like the fishing industry. They claimed that the term fishermen would have a long and proud history, which would not be acknowledged by replacing the term. According to Miller/Swift (1981: 41) it is always possible to respect such desires of some people in individual communication without undermining the purpose of gender-neutral occupation titles but the importance of these new terms is that younger generations have the chance to grow up free from limiting concepts of "men's jobs" and "women's jobs".

4. Generalisations

The problem with generalizations or gender-neutral terms is that even though there is no specific sex-reference present, writers or readers have obviously a specific group in mind. It is very common to find generalizations in which gender is assigned to generic terms like in the following example:

> The typical young adult in Britain is more self-directed, more able to
> make thoughtful choices and grasp unexpected opportunities, than was
> her mother in the sixties.
> (Miller/Swift 1981: 62)

Even if there is no specific reference to sex in the expression the typical young adult most people will surprised or even confused by this generalization phrased in terms of women since adult is largely referred to adult male. The assignment of gender to a generic word is usually less deliberate since the concept of "man" is still more present than the concept of "woman" especially with regard to a profession or a business. Miller and Swift present some examples for which it is not difficult to find an alternative but what they claim is that it is less easy to convince writers of the need to work against their tendency to androcentrism.

5. Non – parallel treatment

There are several areas in which the linguistic treatment of women and men is not equal like the description of both sexes with double standards. This entails the description of women by their outer appearance whereas men are portrayed by their achievement. As soon as there is this emphasis on the physical characteristics of women in contexts where men are described in terms of their character, performance and achievements, writers behave offensive towards women believing that a woman's appearance is incompatible with her capabilities or her competence.

Moreover, women are often described by their relationship to men but men are rarely described by their relationship to women like in the example Margaret Miller, the widow of Ross McDonald, has herself been a prolific writer of mystery stories [...] (Miller/Swift 1981:111). One of the reasons that women are treated as appendages of men goes back to a social custom in the 19th century when it was common to call a married woman by her husband's full name like Mrs Humphrey Ward (Miller/Swift 1981:111). This custom remains especially strong when the women's husbands are known better than they are. However, even if women are known better or are as famous as their husbands or companions, they will be described by their relationship to them as with Simone de Beauvoir, a famous philosopher, writer and feminist who is primarily described by her relationship to the famous philosopher Jean-Paul Sartre. Another aspect of non-parallel treatment is the order of word pairs in which male referents occur first as in fixed collocations like men and women, boys and girls or husband and wife. The convention of placing males first is a deeply embedded habit which can and should be broken by conscious endeavours. Miller and Swift do not offer a real solution if this is possible at all since a change of the order in such word pairs would be nothing else than a non-parallel treatment of men.

Miller and Swift describe further areas in which this aspect of non-parallel treatment is divided into like the treatment of women in religious language or the trivializing of women's behaviour and actions.

4.2.3 Effects and reactions

Miller and Swift were promoting some practical reforms with the intention and effort to encourage writers to think about the effects of their language use. Their handbook was enormous influential and further guidelines were developed that did not only aimed at the elimination of sexist language but focused on the promotion of a bias–

free and non–discriminatory language. However, Miller's and Swift's work and positions as those of many feminists are often criticised for being to simplistic. In their opinion sexist language would distort the truth still representing a world where woman's place was at home, disregarding the contributions and sometimes even the presence of women. Since it would be the business of language to represent reality, changes ought to be made in language in order to bring it into line with the way things really are (Cameron 1992:102). But according to Cameron this point of view is too simplistic since sexism does not just disappear by exposing it in guidelines and no one would have the power to control what people say or mean since "in the mouths of sexist, language can still be sexist."(Cameron 1992:125)

6. Conclusion

Political correctness still remains a controversial topic until today since the majority of people associate different ideas with this term. For many people, it is just a slogan or catchword with a rather ironic meaning, which gained attention when it was taken up by the mass media and some associate the term political correctness explicitly with the invention of rather grotesque neologisms.

However, for those who were directly involved in the political correctness debate like feminist movements, the term represented a moral as well as political position and they connected it with concrete ideas.

Above all, language plays a major role in the political correctness debate. The prevalent assumption, on which the claim for a language change was based, was that language use does not only reflect the social situation e.g. of women but also shapes society. Sexist language, according to this hypothesis, reflects on the one hand a society and worldview, which is dominated by men. On the other hand, children would also acquire aspects of this dominant worldview during their process of language acquisition. Although studies have confirmed that there is a definite relation between language and thinking and that the concept of "men" is still more present in the worldview than that of "women", proposed alternatives have not automatically lead to a change of this worldview. The important distinction is that language has an influence on thinking but that it does not determine our perception. If there was a linguistic determinism this would mean that language would be the main reason for sexist thinking and behaviour and that this problem could only be solved by changing language. It is quite obvious that sexism, racism and other serious problems of humanity were not caused exclusively caused by language use, although language has played a relevant part within these conflicts.

Therefore speech regulations or codes that sanction concerned words are quite controversial since words are always relevant to its context. It is rather difficult to account the insulting connotation of a single lexeme.

Moreover, the majority of people (including myself) use "politically *in*correct" terms unconsciously which does not mean that these people are automatically sexist, racist or intend to offend others. Most of us follow ingrained language habits and are not aware that by saying "Dr. Jones and his wife" we might be regarded as being sexist since we have mentioned "his wife" and not "Mrs Jones" in the second place.

Furthermore, opponents claim that speech regulation would contradict to the freedom of speech which is guaranteed in the First Amendment. Of course, freedom of speech does not mean that all speech is protected. Freedom of speech may not be abused by racist, sexist people in order to insult others.

Finally, who has the power to control what people say and what they mean? And what are we supposed to say nowadays without being sometimes political incorrect when language itself underlies a constant change?

Nevertheless, the whole debate about political correctness, the efforts of feminist to reform language and the introduction of guidelines have led to positive changes. Above all, they have led to an increased awareness for discrimination through language, the cultural diversity in our society and to a more sensitive language use in most cases. Guidelines, which support writers and companies with avoiding sexist language, can be seen as a positive and definitely necessary development.

Still, one must never forget that the simple exposure of sexist language will never be the solution for such a serious problem like discrimination. Those who think that political correctness in the English language would change the feelings and thoughts of people assume that the human consciousness, society and reality are explicitly expressed by language. Those people also assume that the adjustment of language can work wonders which is not the case as Dieter A. Zimmer (Greil 1998:115) maintains by saying "[...] und wer sich von der Sprache Wunder verspricht, kann sie nicht ernst nehmen."

7. References

1. Secondary literature

- Cameron; Deborah (1985) *Feminism $ Linguistic Theory*. London [u.a.]: MACMILLAN PRESS LTD

- Cameron, Deborah (1995) *Verbal Hygiene*. London and New York: Routledge

- Goddard, Angela; Patterson, Lindsay Mean (2007). *Language and Gender*. London [u.a.]: Routledge

- Greil, Tanja (1998) *Political Correctness und die englische Sprache – Studien zu (nicht-) diskriminierenden Sprachgebrauch unter besonderer Berücksichtigung des Social Labelling*.Hamburg: Verlag Dr. Kovac

- Miller, Casey; Swift, Kate (1981) *The Handbook of Non-Sexist Writing – for Writers, Editors and Speakers*. London: The Women's Press

- Möller, Simon (1999) *Sexual Correctness – Die Modernisierung antifeministischer Debatten in den Medien*. Opladen: Leske + Budrich

- Schenz, Viola (1994) *Political Correctness – Eine Bewegung erobert Amerika*. Frankfurt am Main: Peter Lang Gmb - Europäischer Verlag der Wissenschaften

- Wierlemann, Sabine (2002) *Political Correctness in den USA und in Deutschland*. Berlin: Erich Schmidt Verlag GmbH & Co.

- Yule, George (1996) *The study of language*. Cambridge: Cambridge University Press

2. Internet source

- Jacobsen, Carolyn (o.J). Department of English at the University of Pennsylvania. *www.english.upenn.edu/~cjacobso/gender.html*